AF436538

How to Identify a Friend

Adrian Collins

Adrian Collins

First edition
All Rights Reserved
Author: © Adrian Collins

The total or partial reproduction of this book, as well as its transmission by any means, is prohibited without the express written authorization of the author. Any unauthorized use constitutes a violation of copyright.

Copyright holder: © 2024 Julian Velandia

Index

The Value of True Friendship

The value of true friendship is something that is not always appreciated at first glance, but over time it becomes one of the most important things in our lives. A true friendship is one that accompanies us in good and bad times, without judging us, without expecting anything in return, simply being there because they want the best for us. It is a bond that is formed over time, based on trust, respect and sincerity. In a world where we often feel alone or misunderstood, finding someone with whom we can be ourselves is a priceless gift.

True friendship is not based on how many friends we have, but on the quality of those relationships. It's easy to surround yourself with people who share our tastes or interests, but a true friendship goes beyond the superficial. He is the person who listens to us when we need to talk, who supports us when we are down, and who celebrates our successes as if they were his own. This is not someone who is only present during fun times, but someone who remains when things get complicated. This type of friendship gives us a sense of belonging, helps us feel connected to the world and understand that we are not alone in our struggles.

Throughout our lives, we will meet many people. Some will come and go from our lives quickly, while others will remain. True friendships are those that last, those that withstand the test of time and circumstances. No matter how many times we argue or disagree, a true friendship always finds a way to heal and continue. It's a bond that grows stronger with every challenge overcome together. Sometimes difficulties can even make that friendship even stronger, because when someone is willing to be by our side in difficult times, they show how much they care about us.

True friendship is also characterized by reciprocity. It's not just about receiving support, but also about offering it. In a genuine friendship, both people are willing to make sacrifices for the other's well-being. This does not mean that we must sacrifice ourselves to the point of losing our identity, but that we are willing to be understanding, patient and generous when the other needs it. This type of friendship teaches us the importance of giving without expecting anything in return, of being empathetic, and of valuing human connection above all else.

It is important to recognize the value of true friendship because, in a world where material achievements and personal success are often prioritized, human relationships can take a backseat. However, at the end of the day, what truly enriches our lives is not the things we own, but the people we have around us. A true friendship gives us emotional support that nothing else can. It helps us see things from another perspective, find strength in difficult times, and enjoy happy moments more fully.

Furthermore, true friendship is a reflection of who we are as people. The people who choose to be by our side, who accept us with all our flaws and virtues, show us what really matters in life. They remind us that we don't need to be perfect to be loved, that our imperfections make us human, and that it is possible to find someone who loves us just the way we are. This type of acceptance is liberating and allows us to be authentic, without fear of being judged or rejected.

True friendship also has a profound impact on our mental and emotional health. Studies have shown that people with strong friendships tend to be happier, handle stress better, and have higher self-esteem. This is because a true friendship provides us with a safe space where we can express our emotions, share our concerns, and receive the support we need to overcome life's challenges. Knowing that we have someone who cares about us, who is willing to listen to us and offer us unconditional help, gives us a feeling of security and well-being.

In conclusion, the value of true friendship is not measured in the amount of time we spend together, but in the quality of those moments. It is a relationship based on trust, respect and genuine love, which enriches us and makes us better people. Appreciating and caring for these friendships is essential for our emotional well-being and leading a fulfilling life. A true friendship is a treasure that we must value and protect, because it is one of the most precious things we can have in life.

Signs of a Fake Friendship

Identifying a fake friendship can be challenging, especially because we all want to believe that the people around us are sincere and appreciate us for who we are. However, not all relationships are what they seem, and it is important to be aware of signs that may indicate that a friendship is not genuine. Recognizing these signs is crucial to protect ourselves emotionally and to ensure that we are surrounded by people who truly value us.

One of the most common signs of a fake friendship is a lack of reciprocity. In a true friendship, both people care about each other and are willing to support each other at all times. However, in a fake friendship, it may seem that you are always the one who gives the most, who is there when the other person needs help, but when you need the same, that person disappears. A false friend is one who only comes to you when it suits him, when he needs something from you, but he is not willing to return that support when you need it. This lack of reciprocity may be subtle at first, but over time, it becomes an emotional burden that wears down the relationship.

Another sign of a fake friendship is manipulation. A fake friend may try to control or manipulate your decisions, making you feel guilty if you don't do what he or she wants. This type of behavior is toxic because it is based on selfishness and the need to control others. Instead of respecting your decisions and supporting you in your choices, a fake friend may try to influence you to do what is best for them, even if that goes against your own desires or needs. This manipulation can be emotional, such as making you feel bad for not spending time with him or her, or it can be more direct, such as pressuring you to make decisions that you are not comfortable with.

Inconsistency in behavior is also a sign of a fake friendship. A true friend is someone you can trust, someone who is constant in their dealings with you. On the other hand, a fake friend may be kind and affectionate one day, and distant or indifferent the next. This inconsistency can be confusing and emotionally draining, as you never know what to expect from that person. This lack of stability in the relationship is a clear indication that the friendship is not as strong as it should be, and that perhaps the person is not as committed to the relationship as you are.

Another important sign of a fake friendship is a lack of genuine interest in your life. A true friend is interested in your thoughts, feelings, and experiences, and is willing to listen when you need to talk. In contrast, a fake friend may seem uninterested or distracted when you share your problems or joys, or may quickly change the subject to talk about himself. This type of behavior indicates that the person is not really interested in you as an individual, but is only in the relationship for what he can get out of it. A lack of genuine interest can make you feel alone and unappreciated, which is the opposite of what a true friendship should offer.

Constant criticism and lack of support are also clear signs of a fake friendship. A true friend encourages you and supports you, even when you make mistakes. However, a fake friend may constantly criticize you, making derogatory or sarcastic comments that make you feel bad about yourself. This type of behavior is not constructive or helpful, but is intended to lower your self-esteem and make you feel inferior. A fake friend may also minimize your accomplishments or make comments that downplay your successes, rather than celebrating your victories with you. This type of constant negativity can seriously affect your emotional well-being and is a clear sign that the friendship is unhealthy.

Lack of loyalty is perhaps one of the most painful signs of a false friendship. A true friend is loyal and stands up for you, even when you are not around. On the other hand, a fake friend may talk bad about you behind your back or share your secrets with others. This type of betrayal is devastating because it breaks trust, which is the foundation of any friendship. If you discover that someone you considered a friend is spreading rumors or sharing personal information without your permission, it's a clear sign that the person is not a real friend. Loyalty is essential in any relationship, and without it, there can be no authentic friendship.

Finally, a fake friendship is often characterized by a general feeling of awkwardness or stress. If you feel emotionally drained after spending time with someone, or if you constantly worry about what that person thinks of you, the relationship is likely unhealthy. True friendships should make you feel supported, valued and happy, not anxious or stressed. If a relationship is causing you more harm than good, it's important to reevaluate whether that person deserves a place in your life.

In short, the signs of a fake friendship are many and varied, but they all point to the same thing: a lack of sincerity, reciprocity, and loyalty. Recognizing these signs is the first step in protecting your emotional well-being and ensuring that you are surrounded by people who truly appreciate you. Don't be afraid to walk away from a friendship that makes you feel bad or that doesn't contribute positively to your life. True friendships are those that support you, make you feel good about yourself, and help you grow as a person. Identifying and moving away from false friendships will allow you to make space for healthier, more meaningful relationships in your life.

Envy and Selfishness in Friendships

Envy and selfishness are two emotions that can poison any relationship, especially friendships. Although we have all felt envy or acted selfishly at some point, when these attitudes become a pattern within a friendship, they can destroy what should be a relationship based on mutual support and trust. It is important to understand how envy and selfishness manifest themselves in a friendship and how they affect both those who feel them and those who receive them.

Envy in a friendship occurs when a friend can't stand seeing that you have something that he or she doesn't have. It could be that you are successful in your career, that you enjoy a happy romantic relationship, or that you simply feel good about yourself. Instead of being happy for you, an envious friend feels resentment and jealousy. This type of envy is not always obvious; It can hide behind passive-aggressive comments, criticism disguised as advice, or even sudden distancing from the relationship. An envious friend may try to minimize your achievements or make you feel guilty about your successes, instead of supporting you and celebrating them with you.

Selfishness in a friendship manifests itself when a person puts their own interests above those of the friendship. A selfish friend will always seek to get what he wants, regardless of how his actions affect others. This type of behavior can be very subtle at first, perhaps demanding your time and attention without offering the same in return, or making decisions that only benefit him or her without considering your feelings or needs. Over time, this selfishness becomes a burden that drains the energy and joy from the friendship, leaving one party feeling used and undervalued.

The combination of envy and selfishness in a friendship is particularly harmful. A friend who is envious of you and acts selfishly may try to sabotage you in subtle or even direct ways. He may give you bad advice, not support you when you need help, or even secretly enjoy your failures. This type of behavior can be extremely hurtful because it is coming from someone you trust.

Additionally, envy and selfishness can lead to a cycle of negativity within friendships, where it becomes increasingly difficult to share your successes or ask for support without feeling judged or ignored.

A true friendship is based on mutual support, shared joy in each other's successes, and the ability to be there, both in good times and bad. When envy and selfishness get in the way, these core values are compromised. The relationship becomes toxic, where one person is always trying to maintain control or wanting what the other has. Not only does this affect the quality of the friendship, but it can also have a profound impact on your self-esteem and emotional well-being.

It is important to recognize when envy and selfishness are present in a friendship. If you notice that a friend can't be happy about your accomplishments, always finds a way to make everything revolve around him or her, or constantly leaves you feeling unappreciated, it's time to reevaluate that relationship. It's not easy to accept that someone you consider a friend might be acting this way, but it's necessary to protect your emotional well-being.

It is also crucial to reflect on our own behaviors and emotions. We can all feel envy at some point, but the important thing is how we handle those feelings. Envy does not have to destroy a friendship if we are able to recognize it, confront it, and work to overcome it. This requires honesty with ourselves and, in some cases, with the other person. If you realize that you are feeling envious of a friend, it can be helpful to talk about it openly, explain how you feel, and find ways to support each other.

Likewise, it is essential to recognize when we are being selfish and take steps to change that behavior. Selfishness not only harms others, but it also distances us from the people we care about. A healthy friendship is based on balance, giving and receiving, and being willing to make sacrifices for the well-being of the other. If you realize that your actions are harming your friend, it is important to make a conscious effort to be more considerate and to put the interests of the friendship above your personal desires.

Ultimately, envy and selfishness are natural human emotions, but they should not define our relationships. A true friendship is strong enough to overcome these challenges if both people are willing to work at it. However, if you find yourself in a relationship where envy and selfishness are constant and the other person shows no interest in changing, distancing may be necessary to protect your own well-being.

In short, envy and selfishness in friendships are signs that something is not right in the relationship. Recognizing these signs is the first step in addressing the problem, whether by talking openly with the friend, working on your own feelings, or, in some cases, walking away from the relationship. True friendships are based on shared joy, mutual support, and generosity, and it is important to cultivate these qualities both in ourselves and in our relationships.

The Friend Who Always Needs Something

The friend who always needs something is one of the most common and, at the same time, most exhausting figures in our lives. We all know someone like that, that person who seems to only appear when they need a favor, when they require our help, or when they are looking for a solution to their problems. At first, it's natural to want to help, because in a genuine friendship, mutual support is essential. However, when this dynamic becomes a repetitive pattern, where you are always giving and the other person is always receiving, the relationship begins to lose its balance and can become toxic.

This type of friend can be difficult to identify at first, because we all go through times when we need more support than usual. However, the problem with this type of friendship arises when necessity becomes the basis of the relationship. Instead of being a balanced relationship, in which both friends support each other, it becomes a one-sided relationship, where you find yourself constantly solving the other person's problems, while your own needs are left aside. This can be emotionally draining and, over time, can lead to resentment and frustration.

A friend who always needs something may not realize that he or she is abusing the friendship. Often these people have no bad intentions; They are simply used to depending on others to solve their problems. However, this does not mean that you should accept this behavior indefinitely. It is important to recognize when the relationship is becoming unbalanced and take steps to correct it. This is not only necessary to protect your own emotional well-being, but also to help your friend become more self-sufficient and learn to solve her problems on his own.

One of the signs that you are dealing with a friend who always needs something is how often he contacts you only when he is in a pinch. He may not be looking for you to spend time together, to enjoy a conversation or simply to share quality moments. Instead, he only appears when he needs a favor, advice, or someone to get him out of a bind.

This type of behavior is not only exhausting, but it can also make you feel used, as if friendship only exists based on what you can offer, and not because of the value you have as a person.

Another aspect of this type of friendship is that often the friend who always needs something shows no real interest in your own needs or problems. He may listen to you when you talk about your difficulties, but he rarely offers concrete help or support. Instead, the conversation often refocuses on her own problems and what he or she needs. This type of interaction can make you feel like your problems are not important, or that your needs always take a backseat. Over time, this can erode your self-esteem and make you question the value of the relationship.

It is important to understand that friendship should not be a constant burden. A healthy relationship is based on balance, on the ability of both friends to give and receive in equal measure. If you find yourself in a situation where you are always giving, it is essential to set boundaries and communicate your feelings. This doesn't mean you should end the relationship immediately, but it does mean that you need to talk to your friend about how you feel and the need for the relationship to be more balanced. Many times, the other person is not even aware of what they are doing, and an honest conversation can be enough to change the dynamic.

However, it's also possible that your friend is unwilling or unable to change his behavior. In this case, it is important to ask yourself if this relationship is really beneficial for you. You have no obligation to maintain a friendship that makes you feel exhausted, used, or belittled. We all deserve relationships that enrich us, that bring us joy and that make us feel valued. If a friendship isn't meeting these criteria, it may be time to reconsider its place in your life.

Additionally, it is crucial to reflect on why you attract these types of friends. Sometimes people who always give tend to attract those who always need something. While it's noble to want to help others, it's important to remember that your own needs matter too. Learning to say no, set limits and prioritize your own well-being is essential to maintaining healthy and balanced relationships.

In short, the friend who always needs something can be an exhausting presence in your life. While it is natural to want to help, it is important to recognize when this dynamic has become unsustainable. Talking openly, setting boundaries, and, if necessary, reevaluating the relationship are key steps to protecting your emotional well-being and ensuring your friendships are mutually beneficial. A true friendship is one in which both friends support each other, where both feel valued, and where the relationship enriches both parties. Don't be afraid to stand up for what you deserve in a friendship and take steps to ensure your relationships are healthy and balanced.

Friends who don't support your dreams

Friends who don't support your dreams can be a great source of demotivation and frustration in your life. We all have dreams and goals we want to achieve, and it's natural to seek support and approval from the people we care about most, especially our friends. However, we do not always receive that support. Sometimes those we consider friends can consciously or unconsciously discourage us or even sabotage our efforts to achieve what we want. This can be very painful because we expect friends to be our greatest allies on the path to success.

A friend who doesn't support your dreams can express their lack of support in different ways. Sometimes, it can be through derogatory or demotivating comments that make you doubt your own abilities. Phrases like "Are you sure you can do it?" or "That sounds too hard" may seem innocent, but when they come from someone close to you, they can deeply affect your confidence. These comments are often presented as concerns or realism, but in reality, they undermine your enthusiasm and can make you question whether your goals are worth pursuing.

Another way a friend may not support your dreams is by simply ignoring or minimizing them. He may show no interest when you talk about your plans or change the subject quickly, as if what you're saying isn't important. This type of behavior is equally harmful because it makes you feel like your aspirations are invalid or unworthy of attention. We all need to feel like our dreams matter, and when a friend doesn't take the time to listen to you or show interest, it can be very discouraging.

There are times when a friend may even try to derail your plans, offering you alternatives that go against what you really want. For example, if you have a dream of starting a business, a friend might try to convince you to stay in a secure job because he believes it is best for you. Although this type of advice may seem well-intentioned, if it goes against what you really want, it can prevent you from pursuing what you are truly passionate about. It's important to recognize when a friend's advice is based more on their own fears or limitations than on a true desire to help you succeed.

A friendship that doesn't support your dreams can also be based on envy or fear of change. Sometimes a friend may feel threatened by your aspirations, especially if they feel that your achievements could change the dynamic of the relationship or cause you to walk away. This type of friend might subconsciously want to keep you in the same place to avoid feeling inferior or to keep things the way they are. However, a friendship that requires you to sacrifice your dreams to make the other person feel comfortable is not a healthy friendship.

It is essential to surround yourself with people who believe in you and your dreams. True friends are those who encourage you to achieve your goals, who celebrate your achievements and who are by your side when things don't go as you expected. It's not about them agreeing with every decision you make, but it is about respecting and supporting your efforts to follow what you really want. A friend who does not support your dreams may be showing that he does not share your values or that he is not willing to see you grow and evolve.

When you realize that a friend is not supportive of your dreams, it is important to evaluate the relationship and decide how you want to proceed. It can be helpful to have an open conversation about how you feel, expressing your needs and explaining why support is important to you. Sometimes the other person doesn't realize the impact their words or actions have, and talking about it can help change the dynamic. However, you may also discover that the friendship is not what you thought, and that the other person is not willing or able to give you the support you need.

In some cases, it may be necessary to distance yourself from those who do not support your dreams. This doesn't mean you have to cut off the relationship completely, but it does mean that it's important to protect your energy and focus on surrounding yourself with people who push you forward. It is essential to remember that your dreams are valuable and deserve to be respected and supported. Don't let a friend's lack of support discourage you or make you doubt your abilities. Instead, look for relationships that inspire and strengthen you, that motivate you to keep going, even when the going gets tough.

Finally, it is important that you also be that type of friend who supports the dreams of others. Reflect on how you can be a source of encouragement and support to those around you, and be sure to celebrate their successes as much as you would like them to celebrate yours. The strongest and most meaningful relationships are those where both people push each other toward their goals, creating a positive cycle of support and growth. By surrounding yourself with people who believe in you and becoming that kind of friend to others, you will be building a circle of friendship that is not only strong, but also enriching and rewarding.

In short, friends who don't support your dreams can be a significant barrier on your path to success. It is crucial to recognize when this is happening, address the problem directly and, if necessary, make difficult decisions to protect your aspirations. Remember that your dreams are an essential part of who you are and that you deserve to surround yourself with people who encourage you to achieve them. By doing so, you will not only be honoring your own desires, but also building relationships that will lead to a more fulfilling and satisfying life.

Emotional Manipulation in Friendships

Emotional manipulation in friendships is a delicate topic and often difficult to recognize. Manipulation occurs when a person attempts to control or influence another person's feelings, thoughts, or behaviors for their own benefit. In the context of a friendship, this can be especially damaging, since the relationship is based on trust and mutual respect. When one friend emotionally manipulates another, she is violating that trust and distorting the natural balance that should exist in any healthy relationship.

One of the most common forms of emotional manipulation in friendships is the use of blame. A manipulative friend can make you feel guilty for things that are not your responsibility or for situations over which you have no control. For example, you might say things like, "If you were really my friend, you would do this for me" or "You make me feel bad when you don't do what I ask." These types of statements are designed to make you feel like you're failing as a friend, even when that's not the case. By making you feel guilty, the manipulator puts you in a position where you feel obligated to please them, even if that goes against your own desires or needs.

Another emotional manipulation tactic is victimization. The manipulative friend may constantly present themselves as the victim, someone who is always suffering or being mistreated by others. By doing so, he seeks to generate pity or compassion, and expects you to always be willing to help or give in to what he or she wants. This type of behavior can be very subtle, but over time it can make you feel responsible for the other person's emotional well-being, leading you to put their needs above your own. It is important to remember that in a healthy friendship, both people support each other, and there should not be a constant imbalance where one always gives and the other always receives.

The use of silence or emotional withdrawal is another form of manipulation. This type of manipulation occurs when a friend walks away or stops talking to you as a way to punish you for not meeting her expectations. They may stop talking to you, ignore you, or act distant without explaining why, expecting you to feel bad and try to make amends, even if you haven't done anything wrong. This type of behavior is a form of control, as it puts you in a position of uncertainty and anxiety, making you question what you did wrong and how you can fix it. However, what is really happening is that the manipulator is using your fear of losing the friendship to manipulate you into acting the way he or she wants.

There is also manipulation through pressure to conform. A manipulative friend may try to influence your decisions, tastes, or behaviors to align with theirs. This can range from pressuring you to adopt their opinions to making you feel like you must change aspects of your personality to be accepted. They may say things like, "If you were really my friend, you'd think like me," or "You should do this if you want to be part of our group." This type of manipulation can be very damaging to your self-esteem, as it leads you to question your authenticity and change to please others, instead of being true to yourself.

Emotional blackmail is another common tool in manipulation. This occurs when a friend uses your feelings of affection or loyalty toward them to get what they want. For example, he may threaten to end the friendship if you don't do what he asks, or he may suggest that your refusal to comply with her wishes means that you don't care enough. This type of manipulation is especially harmful because it plays on your emotions and fear of losing the relationship. In reality, a friendship that depends on emotional blackmail is not a true friendship, since it is based on control and not mutual respect.

Emotional manipulation in friendships can be difficult to identify because it is often wrapped in a cloak of care or concern. A manipulative friend may present themselves as someone who only wants the best for you, or who is acting in a certain way "for your own good." However, it is important to be aware of how you feel in the relationship. If you constantly feel pressured, guilty, anxious or dissatisfied, you may be being emotionally manipulated. Friendships should make you feel supported, valued and respected, not controlled or manipulated.

Recognizing emotional manipulation is the first step to protecting yourself from its effects. Once you realize that a friend is using manipulative tactics, it is important to set clear boundaries. This may include talking openly with the person about how you feel, and making it clear that you will not tolerate manipulative behavior. If the friend truly values the relationship, he will be willing to change and work to improve the dynamic between you. However, if he continues to manipulate you or denies that there is a problem, you may need to reconsider whether this friendship is really healthy for you.

In some cases, it may be necessary to distance yourself from a manipulative friendship. This isn't easy, especially if you've been around the person for a long time, but it's crucial to your emotional well-being. A friendship based on manipulation is not a genuine friendship, and continuing in such a relationship will only hurt you in the long run. By distancing yourself, you give yourself the opportunity to heal, to regain your self-esteem, and to make space for healthier, more balanced relationships in your life.

In short, emotional manipulation in friendships is a subtle but powerful form of control that can have devastating effects on your emotional well-being. It is essential to learn to recognize signs of manipulation, such as the use of blame, victimization, emotional blackmail, and pressure to conform. By setting boundaries and, if necessary, distancing yourself from the relationship, you protect yourself and create space for friends who respect and value you for who you are. True friendship is based on mutual support, honesty and respect, and should never make you feel less than or controlled.

When Friend Becomes Competition

When a friend turns into competition, the dynamic of the friendship can change significantly, and not always for the better. Competition in friendships is not uncommon; In fact, it is quite common for two people who like each other and share similar interests to feel the need to compare themselves at some point. However, when competition stops being friendly and turns into a desire to outdo each other at all costs, it can cause tension, resentment, and ultimately damage the relationship.

In a healthy friendship, both friends should feel happy about each other's achievements. There should be a shared sense of pride when one of you reaches an important goal, lands a new job, or experiences a moment of success. However, when competition comes into play, this shared joy can disappear. Instead of celebrating the other's success, one friend may begin to feel envy or resentment, thinking that somehow the other's victory diminishes her own worth.

A clear sign that competition is affecting friendship is when you start to notice that conversations revolve around who is better at something. It is no longer about sharing experiences or supporting each other, but about showing who is more successful, who has more achievements or who is more admired by others. This can manifest itself in subtle comments that are intended to downplay the other's achievements or highlight one's own achievements. For example, if you share that you received a promotion at work, your friend might immediately respond with something he or she has recently accomplished, as if he or she has to match or surpass your news.

Another way competition can manifest in a friendship is through rivalry in specific areas of life, such as work, relationships, or even hobbies. Maybe you both work in the same field and one begins to see the other more as a rival than a friend. Instead of supporting each other and sharing advice, they keep information from each other, feel jealous when the other succeeds, and secretly rejoice when the other faces an obstacle. This rivalry can create a tense and unhealthy atmosphere, where each person feels pressured to always be one step ahead of the other, rather than enjoying the friendship.

Competition can also arise in romantic relationships. If both friends are single, there may be a sense of competition over who finds a partner first or who has the most successful relationship. This can be especially difficult if you are both interested in the same person, which can lead to direct conflict and feelings of betrayal. Even if this is not the case, competition in this area can cause resentment, especially if one of the friends feels that she is always in the other's shadow when it comes to relationships.

When competition becomes too intense, it can lead to behaviors that are harmful to the friendship. One friend might start making hurtful comments, try to sabotage the other's efforts, or act in a disloyal way. Instead of supporting each other, they begin to see each other as an obstacle in their own path to success. This attitude is not only harmful to the friendship, but also to the emotional well-being of both, as it creates an environment of mistrust and resentment.

It is important to remember that each person has their own path and that a friend's achievements do not diminish yours. True friendship should not be based on who is better or who is more successful, but on mutual support, understanding and respect. If you feel like competition is affecting your friendship, it's crucial to address the issue openly. Talk to your friend about how you feel and try to find a way to release that tension. Sometimes simply acknowledging the problem can be the first step to solving it.

Additionally, it is helpful to reflect on why you feel the need to compete with your friend. Often, competition in friendships stems from personal insecurities or low self-esteem. You may feel like you need to prove your worth by comparing yourself to others, but this will only lead you to feel dissatisfied and anxious. Instead of competing, work on developing your own confidence and celebrating your achievements without comparing them to others.

It's also important that both friends strive to foster a culture of support rather than competition. This means genuinely congratulating others on their achievements, sharing joys and successes, and being there to support them through difficult times without resentment or envy. A friendship in which both feel safe and valued is much stronger and lasting than one based on competition.

However, if after talking about the problem and trying to change the dynamic, competition is still an issue, it may be necessary to reconsider the friendship. Not all relationships are meant to last forever, and if competition is causing more harm than good, it might be best to distance yourself and focus on surrounding yourself with people who truly support you and celebrate your successes without comparison.

In short, when a friend turns into competition, the friendship can face significant challenges. It is crucial to recognize the signs that competition is affecting the relationship and take steps to address the problem. A true friendship should not be based on who is better or who is more successful, but on mutual support, respect and shared joy. By working to eliminate competition and foster a supportive culture, you can strengthen the friendship and ensure it is a source of happiness and growth, rather than stress and rivalry.

The Friend Who Speaks Badly Behind Your Back

The friend who speaks badly behind your back is one of the biggest betrayals that can be experienced in a friendship. When we trust someone we do so because we believe that person is loyal, that they value our relationship, and that they would never do anything to intentionally harm us. However, when we discover that a friend has been badmouthing us to other people, that trust is broken and leaves us with a deep and painful feeling of betrayal. This type of behavior not only damages the friendship, but also our self-esteem and the way we perceive our relationships in general.

Badmouthing someone behind their back means that the person says negative, critical, or hurtful things when you are not present, with the intention of belittling or discrediting you in front of others. They may do it to gain acceptance in a group, to feel superior, or simply out of envy. Regardless of the reason, this type of behavior reveals a lot about the character of the person doing it. A true friend does not feel the need to speak ill of you when you are not present; On the contrary, he should defend and support you, especially when you are not there to defend yourself.

One of the most damaging aspects of having a friend who talks trash behind your back is the confusion it creates. Maybe, in front of you, this person seems kind, understanding and close, while behind your back he criticizes you or spreads rumors. This creates a situation where you don't know who to trust, and you begin to question whether what you see is real or if there is something else that you are not sensing. This duality in the friend's behavior is a clear sign of disloyalty, and can make you feel insecure in the friendship, constantly doubting the other person's true intentions.

Another serious problem with these types of friends is the damage they can do to your reputation. Words have power, and when someone you consider a friend says negative things about you to other people, it can influence how those people view you. Even if the criticisms aren't true, the simple fact that someone close to you says them can cause others to start questioning your character or seeing you differently. This can affect not only your personal relationships, but also your professional life, as others' perception of you can change due to the malicious comments of this so-called friend.

It's important to recognize the signs that a friend is talking badly behind your back. You may find out what he has said from third parties, which can be painful but revealing. If several people tell you the same thing, there is probably some truth in it. You may also notice changes in the way others treat you, as if they heard something negative about you and now look at you differently. Additionally, if the friend in question acts evasive or seems uncomfortable when you confront certain topics, it may be a sign that he is hiding something.

When you discover that a friend has been badmouthing you behind your back, it's natural to feel hurt, angry, and betrayed. You may be tempted to confront the person aggressively or to return their favor by badmouthing them as well. However, the best way to handle this situation is calmly and maturely. Talk directly to the friend and express how you feel. Tell him that you've heard what he's been saying and that it hurts you that someone you trusted acted that way. Listen to his response and try to understand why he did it, even if you don't justify his behavior.

The friend may apologize and try to make amends. However, it is important to remember that words spoken cannot be taken back, and the damage has already been done. It is crucial to evaluate whether this friendship deserves a second chance or if it is better to distance yourself from someone who has proven to be untrustworthy. Sometimes an apology is not enough to restore trust, and walking away may be necessary to protect yourself emotionally.

It's also helpful to reflect on the relationship in general. Have there been other signs that this person was not a loyal friend? Has he made you feel bad on other occasions, even though he has not spoken badly about you? This may not be the first time you've realized something isn't right in the friendship, and this behavior may just be a manifestation of deeper problems in the relationship. If so, this may be the opportunity you need to reevaluate the friendship and decide if it's really worth continuing.

Sometimes the best decision is to let these types of friends go. Although it may be difficult, it is important to surround yourself with people who support and value you, not those who seek to tear you down when you are not present. True friendship is based on trust, respect and mutual support. A friend who speaks badly about you behind your back does not comply with these principles, and maintaining a relationship with someone like that will only bring you more pain and mistrust in the long term.

On the other hand, these types of experiences can also teach you valuable lessons about the nature of human relationships and about yourself. They can help you be more selective with the people you trust, identify red flags in future friendships, and strengthen your relationships with those who truly deserve your trust. Learning to recognize who your true friends are and who aren't is an important part of personal and emotional growth.

In short, a friend who speaks badly behind your back is one of the most painful betrayals you can experience. This behavior damages trust, affects reputation, and creates an atmosphere of mistrust and confusion in the friendship. It is important to approach the situation maturely, speak directly to the person and evaluate whether the relationship deserves a second chance. In many cases, distancing yourself from these types of friends is the best option to protect your emotional well-being and surround yourself with people who truly value and support you.

Friendships Based on Superficial Interests

Friendships based on superficial interests are those that are built around external and fleeting things, such as social status, money, physical appearance or any other aspect that has no real depth. These relationships often seem exciting and fun at first, as they can be filled with glamorous activities, light conversations, and moments that, on the surface, seem exciting. However, over time, these friendships tend to fade, because there is no genuine connection to sustain them. What seemed to be a strong relationship can reveal its fragility when the superficial interests that sustain it are no longer relevant.

One of the biggest problems with friendships based on superficial interests is that they lack authenticity. When the relationship is based on external things, such as money or popularity, the people involved usually show only a part of themselves, the one they believe is attractive or acceptable to the other. This means that instead of being honest and showing their true selves, they may feel pressured to maintain an image that is not completely real. This can lead to a relationship where both people are acting out, and where there is no real understanding or support for each other.

Another problematic aspect of these friendships is that they tend to be very fragile. When the foundation of the relationship is superficial, any change in those external circumstances can cause the friendship to crumble. For example, if the friendship is based on social status, a change in one of the people's situations, such as losing a job or no longer being part of a particular social group, can cause the friendship to dissolve quickly. The same is true if the relationship is based on physical appearance or participation in certain activities that are no longer possible or desirable over time. Without a solid foundation of shared values and mutual support, these friendships rarely survive life's inevitable changes.

Additionally, friendships based on superficial interests can create a feeling of emotional emptiness. Although they can be fun and exciting on the surface, they often lack the depth and emotional connection that are essential for a true friendship. People in these relationships can feel alone, even when surrounded by friends, because they don't have someone with whom they can share their deepest thoughts and feelings. Instead of feeling supported and understood, they may feel like they are in a relationship that is based on appearances and not a true connection.

It's important to recognize the signs that a friendship is based on superficial interests. If conversations always revolve around trivial or superficial topics, and never delve into more important or personal topics, it is a sign that the relationship may not have the depth necessary to last. It's also a sign if you feel like you have to act a certain way or maintain an image to be accepted in the relationship. If you feel uncomfortable showing your true self or talking about things that really matter to you, the friendship probably isn't as strong as it should be.

Another sign of a friendship based on superficial interests is if the relationship seems to depend on external things, such as the amount of money you have, the type of job you do, or the things you own. If you feel that your friend's interest wanes when you can't participate in certain activities or don't have something to offer in material terms, the friendship is probably not genuine. In a true friendship, people value each other for who they are, not for what they have or can offer in superficial terms.

Furthermore, these friendships are often marked by a lack of support during difficult times. When things are going well, these friends may be present and seem interested. But when you face problems or need emotional support, they may disappear or appear disinterested. This is because the relationship is based on fun and appearances, and not on a true desire to be there for each other in good times and bad. In contrast, a genuine friendship is strengthened in times of difficulty, because it is based on empathy and mutual support, not on what each can gain from the relationship.

It is important to realize that friendships based on superficial interests are not necessarily bad, but they have a limited place and purpose in our lives. They can be fun and provide us with moments of joy, but they should not be the basis of all our relationships. The deepest and most meaningful friendships are those where we feel free to be ourselves, where there is mutual understanding, and where support is not dependent on what we can offer externally.

To build stronger relationships, it is crucial to seek out friends with whom we share core values and with whom we can have meaningful conversations. These are the friends who will be there through good times and bad, and who will accept us as we are, without needing to maintain a facade or meet certain superficial expectations. It is these friendships that enrich us and help us grow as people, providing a sense of belonging and true connection that cannot be found in relationships based solely on the superficial.

In conclusion, friendships based on superficial interests can be entertaining and provide enjoyable moments, but they lack the depth necessary to be truly satisfying and lasting. These relationships, which are built on external and fleeting things, tend to be fragile and leave a feeling of emotional emptiness when circumstances change. It's important to recognize the signs that a friendship is superficial and value relationships that are based on authenticity, mutual support, and respect for who we really are. By doing so, we can surround ourselves with people who truly value us and who are there for us at all stages of life, providing a solid foundation for personal growth and lasting happiness.

How to Cultivate Sincere Friendships

Cultivating sincere friendships is one of the most important aspects of our social and emotional life. A sincere friendship is one in which people value each other for who they are, support each other, and genuinely care about each other's well-being. These relationships are fundamental to our well-being because they give us a sense of belonging, trust, and emotional security. However, building and maintaining a sincere friendship requires effort, time and commitment. It's not something that happens overnight, but with dedication, we can all learn to cultivate friendships that are authentic and lasting.

The first step to cultivating sincere friendships is to be yourself. Authenticity is the foundation of any genuine relationship. This means that you should feel free to show who you really are, without fear of being judged or rejected. Often when we try to please others, we can fall into the trap of acting in a way that does not truly reflect our beliefs, feelings, or personality. However, to form a sincere friendship, it is crucial that the other person knows you for who you are.

When you are authentic, you attract people who appreciate your true essence, which creates a solid foundation for a long-lasting relationship.

Another fundamental aspect of cultivating sincere friendships is open and honest communication. In a sincere friendship, there should be no room for misunderstandings or assumptions. It is important to express your thoughts, feelings and concerns clearly and respectfully. In the same way, you must be willing to listen and understand what the other person has to say. Effective communication involves not only speaking, but also knowing how to listen, show empathy, and be willing to resolve any conflict that may arise. When both people feel heard and understood, trust is strengthened and friendship deepens.

Mutual respect is another pillar of sincere friendships. Respecting a friend means accepting their differences, valuing their opinions, and treating them with dignity at all times. Even if you don't always agree with what he says or does, it is important to recognize his right to have his own perspective and to live his life according to his own values. Respect also means being considerate and avoiding doing or saying things that could hurt others. When both friends respect each other, they feel safe in the relationship and free to be themselves without fear of being criticized or put down.

Trust is the heart of a sincere friendship. Without trust, it is difficult for a relationship to thrive. To cultivate this trust, you need to be honest and keep your word. This means that if you make a promise, you must keep it, and if you say you will do something, you must do it. Trust is also built by being reliable during difficult times. When a friend needs support, whether emotional, physical, or any other form, being there for them strengthens trust between you. Trust is not gained overnight, but it can be lost in an instant, so it is vital to treat it with care and consideration at all times.

A key element to cultivating sincere friendships is reciprocity. A true friendship is not one-way; Both people must be willing to give and receive equally. This does not mean that each gesture must be reciprocated immediately or to the same extent, but it does mean that both parties must feel valued and supported. If one person is always giving and the other is always receiving, the relationship can become unbalanced and create resentment. Reciprocity also refers to sharing time, effort, and emotions in the relationship. When both people make an effort to maintain the friendship, it becomes stronger and more meaningful.

Empathy plays a crucial role in cultivating sincere friendships. Being empathetic means putting yourself in someone else's shoes and trying to understand how they feel and why they act in a certain way. Empathy allows you to connect with your friend on a deeper level, as it helps you understand their emotions and reactions. When you show empathy, your friend feels understood and valued, which strengthens the bond between you. Empathy also helps you respond in a more compassionate and supportive way in times when your friend is going through difficulties, which further strengthens the friendship.

Time and commitment are essential to cultivate a sincere friendship. Friendships don't develop overnight; They require time to grow and mature. It is important to dedicate time to the relationship, whether through conversations, shared activities, or simply being present in each other's lives. Commitment means being willing to invest in the relationship, even when things get tough. All relationships go through ups and downs, but being willing to work on them and overcome challenges together is what separates a sincere friendship from a superficial one. Commitment also involves being there for each other in good times and bad, showing that you value and appreciate the relationship.

Loyalty is another essential component of a sincere friendship. Being loyal means being on your friend's side, supporting them and defending them when necessary. It also means not speaking ill of him behind his back and being willing to defend his reputation when others attack him. Loyalty creates a sense of security in the relationship, as you both know you can trust each other no matter what. A sincere friendship is built on knowing that, no matter the circumstances, your friend will always be there for you, and you for him.

Lastly, forgiveness is an important part of any sincere friendship. No relationship is perfect, and over time, misunderstandings or mistakes are inevitable. The important thing is to be able to forgive and let go of resentment when your friend makes a mistake. Forgiveness does not mean that you ignore what happened, but that you decide not to let that mistake damage the relationship in the long term. Being able to ask for forgiveness when you're wrong and accept forgiveness when it's offered is vital to keeping your friendship strong and healthy. Forgiveness allows both of you to move forward, learn from the experience, and further strengthen your bond.

In short, cultivating sincere friendships requires authenticity, open communication, mutual respect, trust, reciprocity, empathy, time, commitment, loyalty and forgiveness. These qualities create a solid foundation upon which a long-lasting and meaningful relationship can be built. Although it may take time and effort to develop these friendships, the result is a network of support and love that will enrich your life in deep and lasting ways. Sincere friendships not only make us feel loved and valued, they also help us grow as people, providing us with a sense of belonging and a genuine connection with others.

The Art of Communication in Friendship

The art of communication in friendship is essential to building and maintaining solid and meaningful relationships. Communication is the foundation on which a true friendship is built, as it allows people to understand, support and connect on a deeper level. Without effective communication, it is difficult for a friendship to thrive, as misunderstandings, resentments, and disconnections can arise. Learning to communicate clearly, honestly, and empathetically is essential to cultivating friendships that are long-lasting and satisfying.

One of the most important aspects of the art of communication in friendship is the ability to listen. Listening does not simply mean hearing the words the other person says, but paying attention to their meaning and the emotions behind them. It is important to show genuine interest in what your friend is saying and give her the space to express her thoughts and feelings without interruptions. Sometimes, what a person needs is not a solution to their problems, but simply for someone to listen to them and understand them. By showing that you are willing to listen, you show that you value your friend and that you are there for them in good times and bad.

In addition to listening, it is crucial to be honest in communication. Honesty is the foundation of trust in a friendship, and without trust, it is difficult for a relationship to thrive. Being honest means expressing your thoughts and feelings clearly and directly, without hiding what you really think or feel. However, honesty must also be handled carefully. It's important to be honest, but also be considerate and respectful of your friend's feelings. The truth should not be used as an excuse to hurt someone, but as a tool to strengthen the relationship and resolve any misunderstandings that may arise.

Empathy is another key component of communication in friendship. Being empathetic means trying to understand your friend's emotions and perspectives, even if you don't always agree with them. Empathy allows you to connect with your friend on a deeper level, as it helps you see things from their point of view. This not only improves communication, but also strengthens the relationship by showing that you care about what your friend is feeling and going through. Empathy also helps you respond in a more compassionate and supportive way, which can make your friend feel more understood and supported.

Clarity in communication is equally important. Sometimes misunderstandings in friendships arise because people don't clearly express what they want or need. It is crucial to be clear in your words and make sure your message is understood correctly. This means avoiding assumptions and being specific about what you are saying. If you have a concern or problem, express it directly instead of expecting your friend to guess what you're thinking or feeling. Clarity prevents confusion and ensures that you are both on the same page, making it easier to resolve any conflict that may arise.

Respect in communication is also essential. Even in disagreements, it is important to maintain a tone of respect and consideration. This means not interrupting your friend when he is speaking, not raising your voice or making derogatory comments. Mutual respect in communication creates a safe environment where both feel free to express their thoughts and emotions without fear of being judged or rejected. This respect is crucial to maintaining harmony in friendship and to ensuring that any conflict can be resolved constructively and peacefully.

Non-verbal communication is another important aspect of the art of communication in friendship. Sometimes what is not said is as important as what is said. Body language, facial expressions, and tone of voice can communicate a lot about how you feel or what you think. It's important to be aware of these non-verbal cues and make sure they align with what you're saying. For example, if you say you're fine but your body language suggests otherwise, it can lead to confusion and misunderstanding. Being consistent in verbal and non-verbal communication helps avoid misunderstandings and strengthens trust in the relationship.

Another important aspect of communication in friendship is the ability to give and receive feedback. Constructive feedback is a powerful tool for personal growth and relationship improvement. However, it is important that feedback is given respectfully and with the intention of helping, not criticizing. At the same time, it's crucial to be open to receiving feedback from your friend without becoming defensive. Accepting feedback constructively shows maturity and a willingness to improve, which can strengthen friendships.

Time also plays an important role in communication. It is essential to dedicate quality time to meaningful conversations. In modern life, with so many distractions and responsibilities, it can be easy to postpone or minimize the importance of these conversations. However, taking time to talk and connect with your friend is vital to keeping your relationship strong. This can be as simple as setting aside regular time to catch up or making sure conversations aren't just limited to text messages or social media. Conversations face to face or at least over the phone allow for a deeper and more meaningful connection.

Patience is another important quality in communication. Not all conversations will be easy, and you may face challenges trying to express your thoughts or understand your friend's. It is important to be patient, both with yourself and with your friend, and give them the time they need to process what is being said. Sometimes difficult conversations require more time to resolve, and it is important not to rush to conclusions or decisions. Patience in communication allows both parties the space to think, reflect, and respond in a thoughtful and thoughtful manner.

Finally, adaptability is key in communication in friendship. Not everyone communicates the same way, and it's important to be willing to adapt your communication style to accommodate your friend's needs and preferences. This might mean being more direct with some people and softer with others, depending on your personality and communication style. The ability to adapt and adjust your communication depending on the situation and the person demonstrates flexibility and consideration, which can make your friend feel more comfortable and understood in the relationship.

In conclusion, the art of communication in friendship is a continuous process that requires attentive listening, honesty, empathy, clarity, respect, awareness of non-verbal communication, constructive feedback, time, patience and adaptability. By mastering these aspects, you can build and maintain friendships that are strong, sincere, and lasting. Effective communication not only strengthens friendships, but also enriches your life by allowing you to connect more deeply and meaningfully with the people around you. Friendships that are built on solid communication are those that last over time, withstanding life's ups and downs and providing constant, genuine support.

How to Deal with Conflicts with True Friends

Facing conflict with real friends can be a challenge, but it is also an opportunity to strengthen your relationship and grow together. Conflict is a natural part of any friendship as we are all different and sometimes those differences can lead to misunderstandings or disagreements. However, the important thing is not to avoid conflict, but to learn to manage it in a healthy and constructive way. By approaching conflict the right way, you can deepen your connection with your friend and ensure that your friendship comes out stronger on the other side.

The first step in dealing with a conflict with a true friend is to recognize that a problem exists. Ignoring or minimizing conflict will not make it go away; In fact, it can cause the problem to grow over time. It's important to be honest with yourself and your friend about what's bothering you. If something has affected you, it is essential that you express it instead of keeping it to yourself, as unexpressed feelings can lead to resentment and eventually damage the relationship. By acknowledging the conflict, you take the first step toward resolution and demonstrate your commitment to friendship.

Once you have recognized the conflict, it is essential to approach the situation calmly and respectfully. Avoid confronting your friend in a moment of anger or frustration, as intense emotions can cloud your judgment and lead you to say things you later regret. Instead, wait until you feel calmer and more rational before starting the conversation. Remember that the goal is not to win an argument, but to resolve the conflict in a way that benefits both of you. Approaching the situation with an attitude of respect and consideration shows that you value the friendship and are willing to work together to overcome any challenges.

Open and honest communication is key to resolving conflicts with true friends. It is important to express your thoughts and feelings clearly and directly, but also in a respectful way. Avoid making accusations or blaming your friend, as this can make them defensive and make it difficult to resolve the conflict. Instead, focus on how you feel and use first-person statements, such as "I feel hurt when..." or "I'm worried that...". This allows your friend to understand your perspective without feeling attacked, facilitating a more productive and open conversation.

Listening is as important as talking when it comes to resolving conflicts. It is crucial to give your friend the opportunity to express his or her point of view without interruption. Listen carefully to what he has to say and try to understand his perspective, even if you don't agree with it. Sometimes simply listening to and validating each other's feelings can be enough to relieve tension and begin to resolve the conflict. By showing that you're willing to listen, you show that you care about what your friend feels and thinks, which can help restore trust and connection in the relationship.

Empathy plays a fundamental role in conflict resolution. Trying to put yourself in your friend's shoes and see the situation from his perspective can help you better understand his feelings and reactions. Empathy doesn't mean you have to agree with everything your friend says or does, but it does mean that you try to understand where he or she is coming from and why he or she feels a certain way. By being empathetic, you can approach conflict with greater understanding and compassion, which can make resolution easier and make you both feel more understood and supported.

Another important aspect in conflict resolution is the willingness to compromise. You both may have to make compromises to reach a solution that works for both of you. Compromise does not mean that one must give in completely, but rather that both must be willing to find a middle ground where their needs and desires can be met. This may involve being flexible and open to different solutions, as well as being willing to put pride and ego aside to prioritize friendship. By being willing to commit, you show that you value the relationship and are willing to do what it takes to maintain it.

In some cases, it may be helpful to find a solution together. Working as a team to resolve conflict can strengthen your relationship and make you both feel more connected. This could involve sitting down together and discussing different options for resolving the problem, or even seeking help from an impartial third party if necessary. By approaching conflict as a team, you reinforce the idea that you are both on the same side and that the goal is to preserve the friendship, not win an argument.

It is also important to be patient during the conflict resolution process. Not all conflicts will be resolved immediately, and it may take time for both of you to process your feelings and come to a solution. Patience allows you to give your friend and yourself space to reflect on the situation without rushing into making rash decisions. Sometimes time can help calm emotions and see things more clearly, making it easier to resolve the conflict more effectively.

Forgiveness is a crucial component in resolving conflicts with true friends.

Forgiveness does not mean forgetting or minimizing what happened, but rather letting go of resentment and being willing to move on. Forgiveness is an act of liberation for both you and your friend, allowing both of you to leave the conflict behind and focus on strengthening the friendship. By forgiving, you also demonstrate emotional maturity and a willingness to prioritize relationship over conflict.

Finally, it is important to learn from conflicts to prevent them from happening again in the future. Each conflict can be an opportunity for growth both personally and in the relationship. Reflect on what happened and how the conflict was resolved, and consider what you could do differently next time. This reflection allows you to learn more about yourself and your friend, which can strengthen the friendship in the long term. By learning from conflict, you can also develop problem-solving skills and improve communication in the relationship, which can help prevent future misunderstandings and disagreements.

In short, dealing with conflicts with real friends requires honesty, respect, open communication, attentive listening, empathy, willingness to compromise, patience, forgiveness, and a learning attitude. By addressing conflict constructively, you can strengthen your friendship and ensure that you both come out stronger and more connected. Conflicts don't have to be the end of a friendship; On the contrary, they can be an opportunity to deepen the relationship and grow together as friends.

Forgiveness and Reconciliation in Friendship

Forgiveness and reconciliation are two fundamental aspects of any lasting friendship. Throughout a relationship, it is inevitable that misunderstandings, disagreements, or even hurts will arise. However, what really defines the quality of a friendship is not the absence of conflicts, but how they are handled when they occur. Forgiveness and reconciliation allow wounds to heal and strengthen the ties between friends, transforming difficult moments into opportunities to grow together.

Forgiveness begins with the conscious decision to let go of resentment and bitterness that may have arisen from a conflict. It's natural to feel hurt when someone you trust has let you down or hurt you, but holding on to those feelings can do more harm than good. Forgiveness does not mean forgetting what happened or justifying the other's actions; rather, it is an act of personal liberation. By forgiving, you decide not to let the pain of the past control your present or future, and you give yourself the opportunity to move toward a healthier, more balanced relationship.

Forgiveness also involves an act of empathy. It's important to try to understand the reasons behind your friend's actions, without immediately judging them. Sometimes people act in hurtful ways without realizing the impact they have on others. Maybe they were going through a difficult time or facing their own internal struggles. By practicing empathy, you can see the situation from their perspective and realize that we are all human and make mistakes. This understanding can make the act of forgiving easier and more genuine.

Reconciliation, on the other hand, is the process of restoring the relationship after a conflict. While forgiveness can be an individual act, reconciliation requires the effort and willingness of both parties to work toward repairing the friendship. Once you have forgiven, it is important to take the necessary steps to heal the relationship and rebuild trust. This may involve honest conversations about what happened, how both parties felt, and what can be done to prevent the problem from recurring in the future.

Reconciliation is not always a quick or easy process. It takes time, patience and open communication. Both friends should be willing to listen and be heard, without interrupting or judging. It is crucial to create a safe space where you both feel comfortable expressing your emotions and concerns. This type of honest dialogue can be the key to resolving misunderstandings and ensuring that you are both on the same page about how to move forward. Reconciliation is not just about resolving conflict, but also about learning from it and strengthening friendships as a result.

An essential aspect of reconciliation is the restoration of trust. When a friend has failed in some way, it can be difficult to trust them again right away. However, trust is the foundation of any healthy relationship, and it is important to work to regain it. This may involve setting new boundaries or expectations within the friendship and making sure you are both committed to adhering to them. Trust is rebuilt over time, through consistent actions and demonstrating that both are committed to the relationship.

Forgiveness and reconciliation also require humility. Both friends must be able to admit their own mistakes and take responsibility for their actions. This recognition of one's own faults shows maturity and a true willingness to improve the relationship. Humility not only facilitates the forgiveness process, but also creates an environment of mutual respect, where both feel valued and understood. By admitting that no one is perfect and that everyone makes mistakes, you create space for growth and improvement in your friendship.

In some cases, reconciliation may not be possible or desirable. There may be situations where the damage caused is too great or where the relationship has become toxic. In these cases, forgiveness remains crucial, not to restore the relationship, but to allow you to move on without carrying the weight of resentment. Forgiveness in these circumstances means accepting what happened, releasing the negativity associated with the situation, and focusing on your emotional well-being. Sometimes the act of forgiving and letting go can be the best option for both parties, allowing each to follow their own healthier path.

Forgiveness and reconciliation are also valuable lessons that you can apply in other areas of your life. Learning to forgive and reconcile in a friendship teaches you conflict management skills, empathy, and patience, which are useful in all interpersonal relationships. These skills can help you build stronger, more satisfying relationships, both in your personal and professional life. By practicing forgiveness and reconciliation, you become a more resilient person and capable of maintaining deep and meaningful connections with others.

Finally, it is important to remember that forgiveness and reconciliation are ongoing processes. They are not one-time events, but practices that require constant effort. As you face new challenges in your friendships, it is essential to maintain an attitude of forgiveness and be willing to reconcile when necessary. This commitment to mutual healing and growth is what truly strengthens a friendship and makes it last. By valuing forgiveness and reconciliation, you ensure that your relationships not only survive, but thrive and become sources of joy and support throughout your life.

Keys to Durability

Maintaining a lasting friendship is like tending a garden: it requires time, dedication, and constant effort. Friendships, like plants, need to be nurtured and tended to in order for them to grow and thrive. In this chapter, we'll explore some important keys that can help you build and maintain friendships that stand the test of time. From effective communication to empathy and mutual support, these keys are essential for a friendship to not only survive, but flourish over the years.

One of the first keys to durability in a friendship is open and honest communication. Communication is the foundation on which any solid relationship is built. Being able to talk openly with your friend about your feelings, thoughts, and concerns is essential to maintaining a strong and authentic connection. Honesty in communication helps avoid misunderstandings and resolve conflicts effectively. When both friends feel free to express what they really think and feel, the relationship becomes more genuine and resilient to challenges that may arise.

Another important key is mutual respect. Respect is essential in any relationship, and in a friendship, it is what allows both partners to feel valued and appreciated for who they are. Respecting differences of opinion, personal decisions and the limits of others is essential to maintaining a healthy and balanced relationship. Respect also means listening without judgment and supporting your friend in their choices, even if you don't always agree with them. By showing mutual respect, both friends create an environment of trust and security, which strengthens the friendship in the long term.

Empathy is another crucial key to durability in a friendship. Being empathetic means being able to put yourself in someone else's shoes, understand their emotions and be willing to support them in difficult times. Empathy fosters understanding and emotional connection, allowing both friends to feel closer and more connected. Additionally, empathy helps prevent conflicts and resolve them more effectively, as it allows you to see situations from the other's perspective and respond more compassionately. A friendship based on empathy is more resilient to difficulties and better equipped to overcome challenges.

Mutual support is another fundamental pillar for a lasting friendship. In a true friendship, both friends must be willing to offer and receive support when needed. This means being present in good and bad times, and being willing to help others when they need it. Mutual support strengthens the emotional connection and creates a sense of loyalty and commitment in the relationship. Knowing that you can count on your friend in any circumstance strengthens the friendship and makes it longer lasting.

Patience also plays an important role in the durability of a friendship. We are all human and make mistakes; Therefore, it is essential to be patient and understanding of each other's flaws and mistakes. Patience allows you to give your friend room to grow and improve, without rushing to judge or criticize. It also helps you stay calm during conflicts and look for solutions instead of reacting impulsively. A friendship that is built on patience is better able to weather life's ups and downs and stay strong over time.

Commitment is another essential key to maintaining a lasting friendship. A strong friendship requires a mutual commitment from both parties to care for and nurture the relationship. This involves making a conscious effort to stay in touch, spend time together, and be present in each other's lives. Commitment also means being willing to work on the relationship when challenges arise, rather than giving up in the face of difficulties. A friendship that is based on mutual commitment is more likely to survive obstacles and stay strong throughout the years.

Flexibility is another important quality for durability in a friendship. Life is constantly changing, and as you and your friend face new circumstances and challenges, it is important to be flexible and adapt to those changes. This may mean adjusting expectations, being understanding of changes in each other's availability, or finding new ways to stay connected. Flexibility allows you to keep the friendship alive and relevant, even when circumstances change. A friendship that is flexible and adaptable is better able to withstand change and stay strong over time.

Forgiveness, as we have explored in previous chapters, is also a fundamental key to durability in a friendship. We all make mistakes, and at some point both friends probably need to forgive and be forgiven. Forgiveness allows us to leave conflicts behind and move forward, instead of holding on to resentment. A friendship that is based on forgiveness is better able to overcome challenges and stay strong and healthy. Forgiveness also fosters trust and mutual understanding, which strengthens the connection between friends.

Another important key is authenticity. Being authentic means being honest with yourself and your friend about who you are and how you feel. In an authentic friendship, both friends feel free to be themselves, without fear of being judged or rejected. Authenticity fosters a deep, genuine connection, which is essential for a lasting friendship. When both friends feel safe to be themselves, the relationship becomes stronger and more resilient to challenges that may arise.

Finally, time is an essential key to durability in a friendship. Relationships are not built overnight; They require time to grow and develop. Spending quality time together, sharing experiences and creating memories strengthens the connection between friends and helps build a solid foundation for the relationship. As time passes, a well-cared for friendship becomes stronger and more resilient to challenges. By investing time in friendship, you demonstrate your commitment and willingness to maintain the relationship long-term.

In summary, the keys to durability in a friendship include open communication, mutual respect, empathy, mutual support, patience, commitment, flexibility, forgiveness, authenticity, and time. By practicing these qualities in your relationships, you can build and maintain friendships that stand the test of time. A lasting friendship is not the result of luck, but of a conscious and mutual effort to care for and nurture the relationship. By applying these keys, you can ensure that your friendships not only survive, but flourish and become sources of joy, support, and personal growth throughout your life.

Friends who Promote your Personal Growth

Having friends who encourage your personal growth is one of the greatest gifts life can offer. These friends are not only there for you through good times and bad, but they also push you to be the best version of yourself. They support you in your goals, motivate you to exceed your limits and help you discover your true potential. In this chapter, we'll explore why it's so important to surround yourself with people who foster your personal growth, how to identify these friends, and what to do to nurture these valuable relationships.

Personal growth is a continuous process that involves learning, changing and improving over time. We all have areas in which we can grow, whether in our career, in our relationships, or in our emotional development. However, personal growth does not occur in a vacuum; It is often influenced by the people we interact with. Friends who encourage your personal growth are those who challenge you to get out of your comfort zone, inspire you with their own example and provide you with the support necessary so you can achieve your goals.

One of the most important traits of a friend who encourages your personal growth is that they always look out for the best for you. This type of friend encourages you to pursue your dreams, even when the path seems difficult or uncertain. When you share your goals with them, instead of doubting or criticizing, they offer words of encouragement and help you see the possibilities. These friends believe in you, sometimes even more than you believe in yourself, and that faith in your potential can be a powerful engine for your growth.

These friends also provide you with constructive support. Instead of just saying what you want to hear, they give you an honest perspective and help you see things from different angles. This may mean pointing out areas where you could improve or suggesting new ideas and approaches that you may not have considered. Although this type of feedback can sometimes be difficult to hear, it is invaluable to your personal development. Friends who offer you this kind of support are genuinely interested in seeing you grow and aren't afraid to challenge you when necessary.

Another key aspect of friends fostering your personal growth is that they inspire you with their own behavior. These people are often role models in their own lives, as they are also committed to their personal growth and development. By watching how they face their own challenges, how they strive to improve, and how they pursue their goals, you are motivated to do the same. Their example shows you what is possible and encourages you to aim for more in your own life.

In addition to inspiring you, these friends also offer you emotional support on your growth journey. The path to personal development is often full of ups and downs, and it is in those difficult moments that you need someone to listen to you, understand you, and offer you a shoulder to lean on. A friend who encourages your personal growth will be there for you when you face challenges, remind you of your value, and help you maintain the right perspective. This type of emotional support is crucial to maintaining motivation and resilience as you work toward your goals.

It's also important to note that friends who encourage your personal growth are not envious of your achievements. Instead of competing with you or feeling threatened by your success, they are sincerely happy for you and celebrate your victories as if they were their own. This type of friendship is based on mutual support and the belief that the success of one does not diminish the value of the other. By surrounding yourself with people who are happy about your successes, you find yourself in a positive and encouraging environment that encourages you to continue moving forward.

To nurture these types of friendships, it is essential to be reciprocal in support. Just as these friends help you grow, you should also be willing to do the same for them. Offer your support when they need it, celebrate their successes, and be a good listener when they face challenges. Friendships that foster personal growth are two-way relationships where both parties benefit from each other's support. By maintaining a balance in the relationship, you ensure that you both continue to grow together and that the friendship becomes stronger over time.

Another way to nurture these friendships is to look for opportunities to learn and grow together. This may mean sharing books, attending workshops or seminars, or simply having deep conversations about topics that interest you both. By participating in activities that promote personal growth, you not only improve your own development, but you also strengthen your connection with your friend. Sharing learning experiences can deepen the relationship and create a stronger bond based on common interests and the mutual aspiration to improve.

It's important to remember that not all friendships foster personal growth in the same way, and it's okay for some relationships to focus on other aspects of life, such as emotional support or the enjoyment of shared activities. However, it is essential to have at least a few friendships in your life that push you to grow and reach your full potential. These relationships act as catalysts for your development and can have a lasting impact on your life.

Finally, it is essential to reflect on the friendships you currently have and evaluate if they are helping you grow or if, on the contrary, they are holding you back. This doesn't mean you should cut ties with those who don't foster your growth, but it is important to recognize what kind of influence they have on your life. By making a conscious effort to surround yourself with people who inspire you and push you to be better, you put yourself on the path to continued and meaningful personal growth.

In conclusion, friends who encourage your personal growth are an invaluable treasure. They are those who inspire you, support you, challenge you and celebrate your achievements with sincerity. These friendships are essential to your development and help you become the best version of yourself. By nurturing these relationships and being reciprocal in support, you can ensure that your personal growth is accompanied by friendships that are lasting, meaningful, and deeply satisfying.

The Power of Gratitude in Friendship

The power of gratitude in friendship is something that is often underestimated, but it has a profound impact on relationships. Thanking a friend for being there, for her support, for the moments shared, is a way to strengthen the bond that unites you. In this chapter, we'll explore how gratitude can transform a friendship, making it stronger and longer-lasting, and why it's important to express our appreciation on a regular basis.

Gratitude in friendship is not just about saying "thank you" when someone does something for you, but about recognizing and valuing that person's presence and actions in your life. When you thank a friend, you are telling him that his friendship is important to you, that what he does makes a difference, and that his company is something you deeply value. This simple act of recognition can have a powerful effect on the relationship, making both of you feel more connected and appreciated.

One of the most important aspects of gratitude is that it reinforces positivity in the relationship. By expressing gratitude, you focus on the good that your friend brings to your life, which in turn helps you see the relationship in a positive light. This focus on the positive not only makes you feel better about the friendship, but it also encourages your friend to continue being a positive influence in your life. Gratitude creates a cycle of positivity that strengthens friendship and makes it more resistant to conflict or misunderstanding.

Furthermore, gratitude has a deep emotional effect. When you thank someone sincerely, it makes them feel valued and appreciated, which can increase their self-esteem and emotional well-being. Knowing that her actions and presence have a positive impact on your life can make your friend feel more motivated to continue being a good friend and invest in the relationship. Gratitude, then, not only benefits the person who expresses it, but also the person who receives it.

It is important to note that gratitude does not always have to be expressed verbally. Sometimes actions speak louder than words.

Showing gratitude to a friend can be as simple as returning a favor, being there when they need you, or surprising them with a kind gesture. These actions show that you value the friendship and are willing to make an effort to maintain it. By showing gratitude through your actions, you are building a solid foundation for a lasting friendship.

Another important aspect of gratitude in friendship is that it can help overcome conflicts. In any relationship, it is normal for disagreements or misunderstandings to arise. However, if both friends have a habit of expressing gratitude, it is easier to resolve these conflicts constructively. Gratitude acts as a reminder of what is important in the relationship and why problems are worth resolving. When both parties feel appreciated, they are more willing to find solutions and work together to maintain the friendship.

It is also important to learn to thank friends for the little things. Often, we focus on the big gestures and forget that it's the small, everyday actions that really build a friendship. A message of support, a call to check on you, an invitation to spend time together, these are all things that deserve to be recognized and appreciated. By expressing gratitude for these little things, you're showing that you pay attention to and value every detail of the friendship.

Gratitude also plays a crucial role in maintaining humility in friendship. When you recognize and appreciate what your friend does for you, you remind yourself that you are not alone and that you don't have it all under control. It is a recognition that you need other people in your life and that their help and support are valuable. This humility is key to maintaining healthy and balanced relationships, where both parties feel equally valued and respected.

Thanking a friend also strengthens trust in the relationship. When you express your gratitude, you are being vulnerable by acknowledging that you depend on that person to some extent. This vulnerability, far from being a weakness, strengthens the trust between you as it shows that you feel comfortable enough to be honest about your feelings. As trust grows, friendship becomes deeper and more meaningful.

It is important to mention that gratitude can also help heal wounds in friendship. If there has been some type of conflict or estrangement, a simple gesture of gratitude can be the first step toward reconciliation. By thanking your friend for something positive he or she has done, you are opening the door to a larger, more constructive conversation about how to improve the relationship. Gratitude can act as a bridge that helps bridge gaps and restore harmony in friendship.

Finally, it is important that the gratitude be sincere. Empty words or forced gestures do not have the same impact as a genuine thank you. For gratitude to truly strengthen friendship, it must come from the heart. Take time to reflect on what you really appreciate about your friend and express it honestly. When gratitude is authentic, it has the power to transform friendship into something deeper and lasting.

In short, the power of gratitude in friendship is immense. It is a simple but effective tool to strengthen the bond between friends, promote positivity and emotional well-being, and overcome conflicts. Through gratitude, you can show your friends how much you value and appreciate them, and in doing so, build stronger, more meaningful relationships. Don't underestimate the impact a simple "thank you" can have on your life and the lives of those around you.

How to Choose and Take Care of Your Friendships

Choosing and caring for your friends is one of the most important decisions you can make in life. The people you surround yourself with have a profound impact on your well-being, your personal growth, and how you face everyday challenges. This chapter focuses on how to choose the friendships that truly add value to your life and how to care for them so that they remain strong and meaningful over time.

Choosing a friendship is not something that should be done lightly. It is important to reflect on what you are looking for in a friend. Some people may prefer friends who share their interests, while others look for someone who complements them or challenges them to be better. The most important thing is that you choose people who respect and value you for who you are, who are there to support you through good times and bad, and who are not afraid to be honest with you, even when the truth is difficult to hear. A friendship based on mutual respect and honesty has a solid foundation to grow.

Once you have chosen your friends, it is essential to take care of those relationships. Caring for a friendship requires effort and dedication. It's not enough to choose your friends well; You must also invest time and energy to keep the relationship alive. This means being present, both in good and bad times. It's easy to be a good friend when everything is going well, but it's during difficult times that friendships are truly tested. Showing support, listening, and offering help when needed are key ways to show that you care and value the friendship.

Communication is another essential aspect to take care of your friendships. It is important to maintain an open and honest dialogue with your friends. If something bothers you or worries you, talk about it. Avoid accumulating resentments or misunderstandings that could damage the relationship over time. Likewise, if your friend says something that hurts you or that you don't like, try to understand his point of view before reacting. Effective communication is the foundation of any healthy relationship, and learning to communicate clearly and respectfully will strengthen your friendship.

It's also crucial to be aware of the expectations you have in your friendships. Sometimes we expect our friends to be perfect, to always be available, or to understand what we need without us telling them. However, we are all human and make mistakes. It's important to have realistic expectations and accept that friends, like anyone, have their own limitations and challenges. Learning to accept your friends as they are, with their strengths and weaknesses, is a key part of maintaining a healthy friendship.

Taking care of your friendships also means recognizing and respecting the limits of others. We all need time for ourselves, and it's important not to demand too much from our friends. While it is essential to be there for them, we must also respect their space and time. Don't expect your friends to be available 24 hours a day, or feel bad if they need some time to themselves. By respecting other people's boundaries, you show that you value their well-being as much as your own, which is essential for maintaining a balanced friendship.

In addition to respecting boundaries, it's important to make an effort to maintain connection. With the fast pace of life, it's easy to lose touch with friends, especially if they live far away or have busy lives. However, a true friendship is not based on how often you see each other, but on the quality of time you spend together. Make sure you make an effort to keep in touch, whether through calls, messages or visits where possible. Keeping the connection alive is essential so that the friendship does not cool over time.

Another fundamental aspect to take care of your friendships is to be a good listener. Often, we are so focused on our own problems and worries that we forget to really listen to our friends. Being a good listener means paying attention to what your friend is telling you, not only with your ears, but also with your heart. Listening with empathy and without judgment is one of the most powerful ways to strengthen a friendship. Sometimes all a friend needs is for you to listen, to give them the space to express their thoughts and feelings without interruptions or unsolicited advice.

It is equally important to show gratitude towards your friends. Thanking your friends for being in your life, for small and big gestures, is a way to strengthen the relationship. We often take for granted the things our friends do, but a simple "thank you" can have a big impact. Gratitude creates an environment of positivity and strengthens the bond that unites you. Don't wait for a special day to show your appreciation; do it at any time, because every day is an opportunity to strengthen your friendships.

Last but not least, caring for a friendship also means knowing when to let go. Not all friendships are meant to last forever, and that's okay. Sometimes people change, grow in different directions, or simply no longer have the same needs or interests. Learning to recognize when a friendship is no longer benefiting you and making the decision to walk away is an important part of self-care. It's not about abandoning friends, but about understanding that not all relationships are forever and that it's okay to move on when necessary.

In short, choosing and caring for your friendships is an ongoing process that requires reflection, effort, and a good dose of empathy. It's not just about finding friends, it's about being a good friend and maintaining the relationships that really matter. By investing time and energy in your friendships, you are building a network of support and affection that will accompany you throughout life. True friendships are one of the greatest riches we can have, and taking care of them is one of the best investments you can make for your emotional and personal well-being.

www.ingramcontent.com/pod-product-compliance
Lightning Source LLC
Chambersburg PA
CBHW051215160726
47994CB00002B/613